CBD!

CBD!

Amy Sohn

Illustrated by Eric Hanson

OR Books
New York · London

© 2019 Amy Sohn
Illustrations © Eric Hanson

All rights information: rights@orbooks.com
Visit our website at www.orbooks.com

First printing 2019

All rights reserved. No part of this book may be reproduced or transmitted in any form or by any means, electronic or mechanical, including photocopy, recording, or any information storage retrieval system, without permission in writing from the publisher, except brief passages for review purposes.

Cataloging-in-Publication data is available from the Library of Congress.
A catalog record for this book is available from the British Library.

Typeset by Lapiz Digital.

Published by OR Books for the book trade in partnership with Counterpoint Press.

hardcover ISBN 978-1-949017-23-6 • ebook ISBN 978-1-949017-24-3

10 9 8 7 6 5 4 3 2 1

Printed in Canada

C P-T N-L CBD.

P-T E-S A B-Z P-T.

B-4 CBD, P-T Y-S E-L:IBS, R-3-8-S, ADHD.

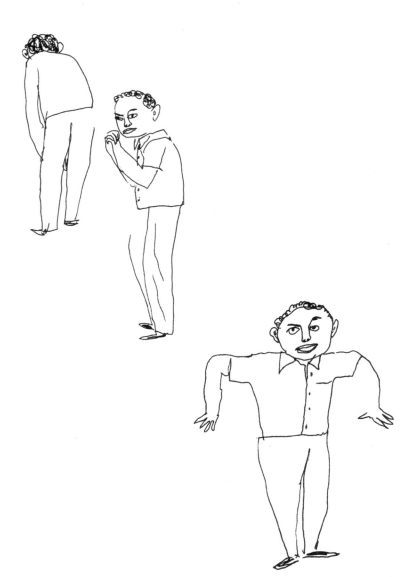

"O-E 1 U 2 B B-8-R," K-T, D Y-F, Z-8.

P-T V-C-T N MD, L-N-R.
"U R A-L-N?"

"S. IBS, R-3-8-S, ADHD."

"CBD K-N B 4 U.
CBD E-S N K-N-A-B-S."

"U K-N E-8 CBD N Q-K & π."

"U K-N F CBD N K-O-F-V."

"CBD E-S 4 A-X N D N-S."

"CBD E-S M-A-Z-N.
CBD E-S D Q-R 4 U."

"S A I?"

"THC S. CBD S-N N-E I.
I K-N E-M-L U A K-N-A-B-S L-I-¢."

P-T 2-K D K-R-D 2 A D-S-P-N-C-R-E.

D D-S-P-N-C-R-E Y-S U-H.

JJ @-D S-M-A. L-C @-D PMS.
V-V-N Y-S N-K-J-S.

"I 1-S 8 MDMA. Y-T N A-R-R."

P-T S-O CBD & THC. O-Y-L, P-L,
F-A-P-R P-N.

F-R-E ᴀ.ᴍ., P-T N-L-T CBD.

@ D O-F-S, P-T @-D N-R-G.
"U R-N S T-S-T."

@ D-N-R,
D F-M-L-E Y-S J-O-K-N & L-A-F-N.
P-T L-I-K-T D G-K-N.

O-N P-T R-8 B-U-X 2 A-M-N,
E D-10 P-K @ E-S I-F-O-N.

E R-8 O-L D Y-A 2 D N-D-N.
"U F B-@-R A-10-J-N."
"I N-O."

P-T N A-M-N P-L-8 4 R-S.

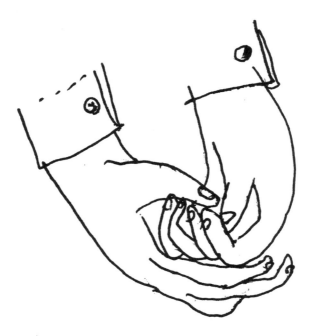

P-T D-T-N Z-A,
"D R-3-8-S, O, D P-A-N!"

B-4 CBD, P-T Y-J-D V-I-L-N,
F-R-I-10-N J-O-S.

F-T-R CBD, P-T & K-T S-@.
P-T L-D K-T 2 E-M.

L-8-R, D-A M-8 D-R-T, 6-E,
L-O-F, O-F-R & O-F-R.
E 8 R D Y-A E 1-S D-T.

"7-L-E!"

F-R-E-T-N Y-S B-@-R 4 K-T, P-T,
N A-M-N.

1 D-A, K-T Z-8 2 P-T,
"I A-F 2 M-N-E P-L-S: F-X-R. M-B-N.
I 1 2 B B-@-R. I 1 CBD."

"CBD S-N 4 U. U 1 THC."

TRANSLATION

1 See Petey inhale CBD.

2 Petey is a busy Petey.

4 Before CBD, Petey was ill: IBS, arthritis, ADHD.

6 "We want you to be better," Katie, the wife, said.

7 Petey visited an MD, Eleanor. "You are ailing?"

8 "Yes. IBS, arthritis, ADHD."

9 "CBD can be for you. CBD is in cannabis.

10 "You can eat CBD in cookie and pie."

12 "You can have CBD in coffee."

13 "CBD is for aches in the hands."

14 "CBD is amazing. CBD is the cure for you."

15 "Has a high?"

16 "THC has. CBD hasn't any high. I can email you a cannabis license."

17 Petey took the card to a dispensary.

18 The dispensary was huge.

20 JJ had asthma. Elsie had PMS. Vivian was anxious.

21 "I once ate MDMA. What an error."

22 Petey saw CBD and THC. Oil, pill, vapor pen.

23 Every morning, Petey inhaled CBD.

24 At the office, Petey had energy. "You aren't as testy."

25 At dinner, the family was joking and laughing. Petey liked the chicken.

26 When Petey read books to Eamon, he didn't peek at his iPhone.

27 He read all the way to the ending. "You have better attention." "I know."

29 Petey and Eamon played for hours.

30 Petey didn't say, "The arthritis, oh, the pain!"

31 Before CBD, Petey watched violent, frightening shows.

32 After CBD, Petey and Katie sat. Petey held Katie to him.

33 Later, they made dirty, sexy love, over and over. He ate her the way he once did it.

34 "It's heavenly!"

36 Everything was better for Katie, Petey, and Eamon.

37 One day, Katie said to Petey, "I have too many pills: Effexor. Ambien. I want to be better. I want CBD."

38 "CBD isn't for you. You want THC."

Amy Sohn

Amy Sohn is the bestselling author of the novels *Prospect Park West, Motherland, My Old Man, Run Catch Kiss*, and *The Actress*. Her books have been published in ten languages and on five continents.

Her well-known, controversial columns at *New York Press,* the *New York Post,* and *New York* put her on the national media landscape. According to *The New York Times,* "A little-known event that took place around the time that Richard M. Nixon was resigning as President was the birth of Amy Sohn, who has emerged as a representative of her generation… There is something about her career so far that suggests a mini-Zeitgeist."

Her articles on relationships, feminism, sex, pop culture, and motherhood have appeared in *The Awl, The Nation, Harper's Bazaar, Men's Journal, Playboy, Playgirl, Elle, The New York Times, Allure*, and many other publications.

She has written pilots for such networks as ABC, Fox, Lifetime, and HBO. She lives in Brooklyn.

Eric Hanson

Eric Hanson's illustrations have appeared in *The New Yorker, The New York Times, Vanity Fair, Rolling Stone, Spy,* and other publications, and on book covers for Knopf, NYRB, HarperCollins, Hachette, Farrar Straus, Chronicle, and OR Books. His stories and satires have been published by *McSweeney's* (15, 17, 27), *The Atlantic, The Paris Review, The Mockingbird, New York Tyrant, Torpedo, The Lifted Brow,* and others. He is the author of *A Book of Ages* (Random House, 2008). His art can be found at www.er-h.com.